STEM IN THE SUMMER OLYMPICS

THE SCIENCE BEHIND
VOLLEYBALL

by Jenny Fretland VanVoorst

pogo

Ideas for Parents and Teachers

Pogo Books let children practice reading informational text while introducing them to nonfiction features such as headings, labels, sidebars, maps, and diagrams, as well as a table of contents, glossary, and index.

Carefully leveled text with a strong photo match offers early fluent readers the support they need to succeed.

Before Reading

- "Walk" through the book and point out the various nonfiction features. Ask the student what purpose each feature serves.
- Look at the glossary together. Read and discuss the words.

Read the Book

- Have the child read the book independently.
- Invite him or her to list questions that arise from reading.

After Reading

- Discuss the child's questions. Talk about how he or she might find answers to those questions.
- Prompt the child to think more. Ask: Volleyball players use thrust when they spike the ball. What other sports use thrust?

Pogo Books are published by Jump!
5357 Penn Avenue South
Minneapolis, MN 55419
www.jumplibrary.com

Copyright © 2020 Jump!
International copyright reserved in all countries. No part of this book may be reproduced in any form without written permission from the publisher.

Library of Congress Cataloging-in-Publication Data

Names: Fretland VanVoorst, Jenny, 1972- author.
Title: The science behind volleyball / by Jenny Fretland VanVoorst.
Description: Pogo Books Edition. | Minneapolis, Minnesota: Jump!, Inc., [2020] | Series: STEM in the Summer Olympics | Audience: Ages: 7-10. Includes bibliographical references and index.
Identifiers: LCCN 2019004541 (print)
LCCN 2019009245 (ebook)
ISBN 9781641289160 (ebook)
ISBN 9781641289146 (hardcover: alk. paper)
Subjects: LCSH: Volleyball–Juvenile literature. Sports sciences–Juvenile literature. Olympics–Juvenile literature.
Classification: LCC GV1015.34 (ebook)
LCC GV1015.34 .F74 2020 (print) | DDC 796.325–dc23
LC record available at https://lccn.loc.gov/2019004541

Editor: Susanne Bushman
Designer: Michelle Sonnek

Photo Credits: monticello/Shutterstock, cover (volleyball); Anton Starikov/Shutterstock, cover (clipboard); LEON NEAL/Getty, 1; YASUYOSHI CHIBA/Getty, 3; PEDRO UGARTE/Getty, 4, 10; Xinhua/Alamy, 5; Foto Arena LTDA/Alamy, 6-7, 15, 18-19; PHILIPPE LOPEZ/Getty, 8-9, 16-17; CP DC Press/Shutterstock, 11, 14, 20-21, 23; PA Images/Alamy 12-13.

Printed in the United States of America at Corporate Graphics in North Mankato, Minnesota.

TABLE OF CONTENTS

CHAPTER 1

BUMP! SET! SPIKE!

Let's play volleyball! It is a popular sport around the world. It has been part of the Olympics since 1964.

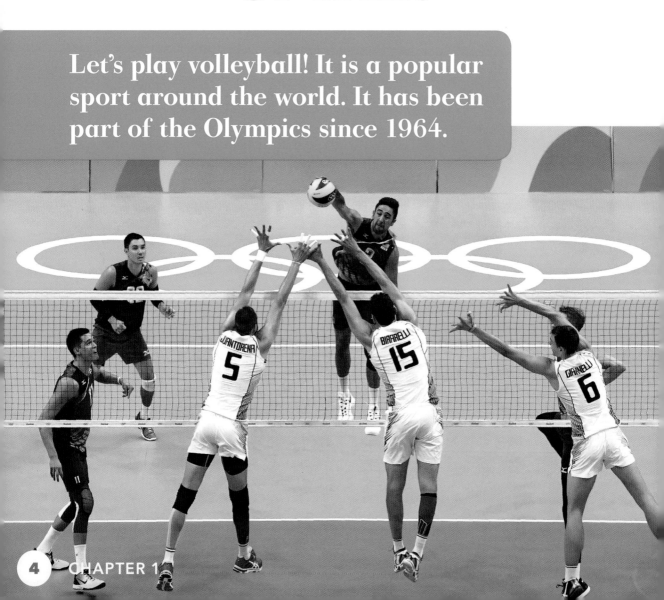

Olympic volleyball players are some of the best. Did you know they use **physics** to win medals?

gold medal

Volleyball players understand the **forces** acting on the ball's flight. They use them to control the ball.

This player jumps up above the net. He spikes the ball down! He applies force to move the ball. This is **thrust**. **Drag** works against thrust. It slows the ball's flight.

DID YOU KNOW?

There are two Olympic volleyball events. Beach and indoor. There are many differences between the two. Like what? The scoring, court size, number of players, and size and firmness of the ball are all different.

spike

net

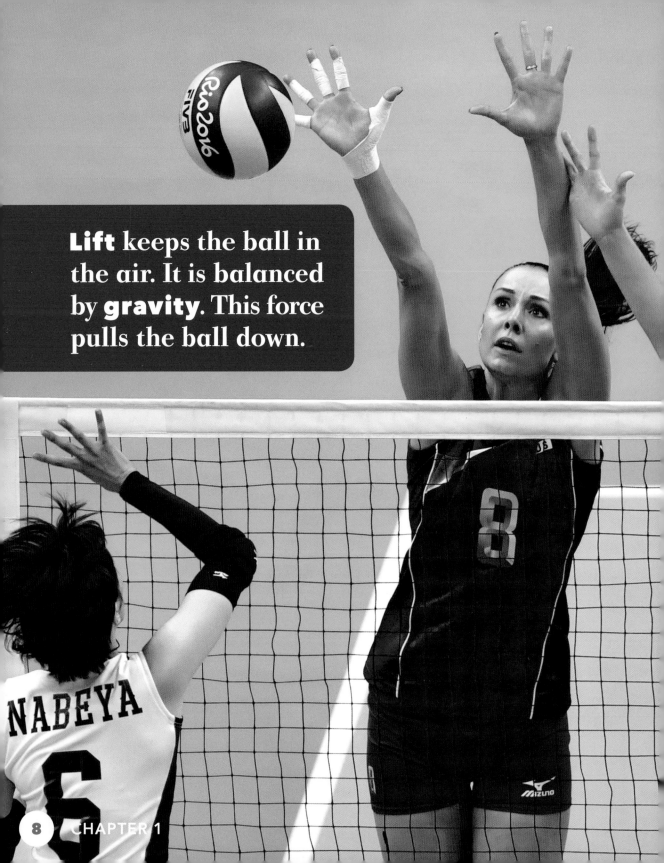

Lift keeps the ball in the air. It is balanced by **gravity**. This force pulls the ball down.

TAKE A LOOK!

Four forces act on a volleyball when it is in the air. Take a look!

gravity

drag

thrust

lift

CHAPTER 2

START WITH A SERVE

Olympians use physics when they serve. How? One way is by applying **topspin**. The server tosses the ball up. She snaps her wrist and sends the ball over the net.

The ball spins forward as it flies. Lift quickly decreases. The ball drops just past the net. Topspin is a fast serve. But it is **predictable**. The other team knows what the ball will do.

The float serve is unpredictable. The server tosses the ball up. She jumps and slaps it flat with the palm of her hand. The ball does not spin. Drag and lift affect the flight differently each time. The other team cannot predict where the ball will land. In beach volleyball, the wind makes the ball's path even harder to predict.

DID YOU KNOW?

As of 2019, the fastest serve on record was 83 miles (134 kilometers) per hour! Zoom!

float serve

CHAPTER 3

MOTION IN ACTION

Volleyball is fast-paced. The players **volley** back and forth. Bump. Set. Spike! Score!

bump

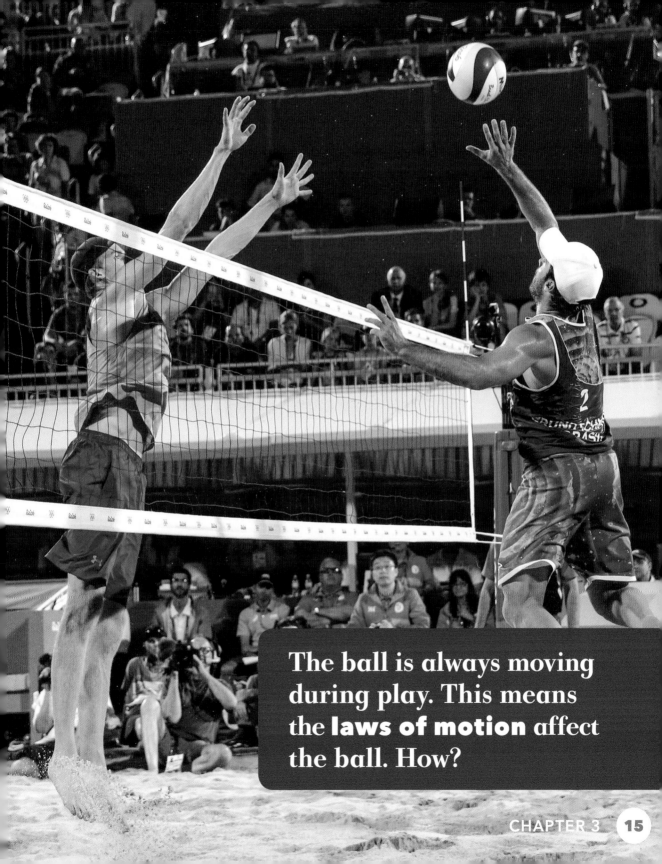

The ball is always moving during play. This means the **laws of motion** affect the ball. How?

block

A player serves the ball. The ball flies in a low arc over the net. Why? A moving object moves in one direction. It only changes if another force acts on it. The ball clears the net.

But wait! A player on the other team jumps. She blocks the ball. Her force changes the ball's path.

The ball goes back across the net. The setter sets the ball. Her teammate jumps to spike it.

DID YOU KNOW?

As of 2019, the highest jump in Olympic volleyball was made by Leonel Marshall. He played for Cuba. He jumped 4.2 feet (1.3 meters) into the air!

setter

DANI LINS

3

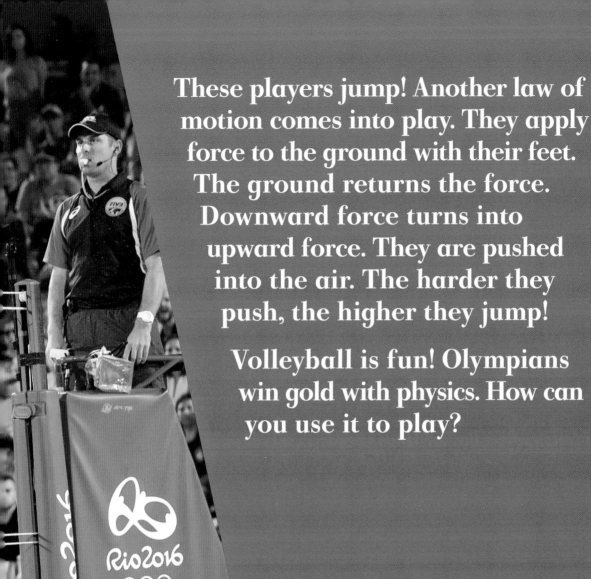

These players jump! Another law of motion comes into play. They apply force to the ground with their feet. The ground returns the force. Downward force turns into upward force. They are pushed into the air. The harder they push, the higher they jump!

Volleyball is fun! Olympians win gold with physics. How can you use it to play?

ACTIVITIES & TOOLS

TRY THIS!

SERVE UP SOME FUN!

Try some different serves to see how well you can control a volleyball's path.

What You Need:
- a volleyball
- a large, open area
- items for marking
- a friend

Try the following serves. Ask a friend to mark where the ball lands after each serve.
- **Underhand:** Hold the ball at waist level with one hand. Hit the ball from below with the flat fist of the other hand.
- **Overhand:** Hold the ball above your head with one hand. Then hit it from behind with the flat fist of your other hand.
- **Overhand with Topspin:** Hold the ball above your head with one hand. Then hit it from behind with the open palm of the other hand. Flick your wrist down as you hit the ball.
- **Float:** Throw the ball above your head, jump up, and smack it with your open palm.

Repeat each serve several times. Did the kind of serve change the ball's flight path? Or how far it flew? What conclusions can you draw from your findings?

GLOSSARY

drag: The force that slows or blocks motion or advancement.

forces: Actions that produce, stop, or change the shape of movements or objects.

gravity: The force that pulls objects toward the center of Earth and keeps them from floating away.

laws of motion: The three laws of physics that govern moving objects, such as every action has an equal and opposite reaction, that were discovered by Isaac Newton.

lift: The upward force that opposes the pull of gravity.

physics: The science that deals with matter, energy, and their interactions.

predictable: Behaving in a way that can be expected and anticipated.

thrust: The force that drives a person or object forward.

topspin: A hit that causes the ball to rotate forward after it is hit, creating a downward force.

volley: To pass a volleyball back and forth over a net.

INDEX

TO LEARN MORE

Finding more information is as easy as 1, 2, 3.

1 Go to www.factsurfer.com

2 Enter "sciencebehindvolleyball" into the search box.

3 Choose your book to see a list of websites.

FACT SURFER